Galway Travel Guide

Sightseeing, Hotel, Restaurant & Shopping Highlights

Thomas Austin

Table of Contents

Galway

On the west coast of Ireland is the beautiful county of Galway with its famous Connemara mountains and rocky coastline. The university city of Galway is a typical Irish city of music and merriment with an atmosphere of culture and sport and is known as Ireland's cultural heart.

The Connemara National Park includes the picturesque Kylemore Abbey with its Victorian walled gardens. Just a short ferry ride away is the Aran Islands where you will find a land that time forgot.

The eastern part of County Galway is a contrast to the west with a flat landscape and many rivers and small lakes. Lough Corrib is where County Galway meets County Mayo and is the largest lake in the Republic of Ireland where you can take a cruise on the smooth waters.

To the north of the county is Clifden, the main town of the Connemara region. The town became famous when Guglielmo Marconi chose to build his fixed wireless service here in 1905. It was to be the first point-to-point communication between North America and Europe and opened to the public in 1907 with a 10,000 word transmission. Marconi chose Clifden as it was the closet point to Glace Bay where the sister station was. At one point over 400 people were employed by Marconi in Clifden.

Galway City is full of historical and cultural buildings and areas of interest, many dating back to early Christian times. Many have been well preserved. Galway has produced many great artistic and literary greats and the history of these people lives on in the city.

Shopping in Galway City means browsing around a mixture of large or small stores, looking at handmade or man-made items, both ancient and modern. From the big brand stores to many local handicraft shops there is whole wealth of goods waiting to tempt you. Around every corner there is a new bookshop or boutique with attractive window displays hoping to entice passers-by in.

The main shopping areas are the pedestrianised streets round Quay Street then the Latin Quarter, Eyre Square and Dominick Street. In Dominick Street the Bridge Mill has been converted into a small shopping centre with gift and craft shops as well as a coffee shop, wine bar and art gallery. Kirwan's Lane is an excellent example of architecture from the 16th and 17th centuries and this mediaeval treasure is lined with craft shops and individual shops as well as several restaurants and bars.

The Saturday Market between Shop Street and Market Street is a well patronised market come rain or shine. Locals and visitors rub shoulders as they jostle each other to see the wide variety of fresh fruit and vegetables, herbs and fresh baked goods on display. The sound of sausages sizzling adds to the generally buzz of the market with stall-holders and customers vying with each other to make the most noise.

Proof that Galway has been inhabited for many years came to light when evidence of shellfish middens were discovered. Oysters were a very popular food source in Roman times and the proximity of oyster beds made certain places worth developing into towns. By the twelfth century, the Normans were in control and in 1270 they built walls round the city as defences. International trading then began with ships sailing to and from the West Indies and Spain. The Spanish Arch in Galway City is a sign of the influence the Spanish had on the town.

Culture

When arriving in Galway City a good way to get a feel for the place would be to take an organised bus tour. Galway City Tours offer a hop-on hop-off system that takes in up to 25 of the best attractions and highlights of the city. http://www.galwaybustours.ie/. Through the daytime the streets will be thronged with shoppers and workers going about their business. By early afternoon the pubs start to fill up as young and old come out for a pint of the black stuff. When the pubs close the partying spills out into the streets and can carry on until early morning.

The university city of Galway has an atmosphere of culture and outdoor activities and national sports and is known as Ireland's Cultural Heart. There are plenty of social activities in the numerous bars, pubs and clubs where traditional Irish music and hospitality can found all day and night. There are festivals and events for nearly everything in County Galway, walking, marathons, cycling, mussels, fishing, football, canoe polo, a bog festival, currach racing, films, food, quilts and hurling, the list is pretty endless. If you are in Ireland in March be sure not to miss a St Patricks day event somewhere. www.stpatricksfestivalgalway.com

There are art weeks, culture weeks and also live entertainment weeks where up to 50 musicians perform in and around the city. Within the city there are approximately 50 event venues with the main ones being Spanish Parade next to the Spanish Arch and Eyre Square containing John F. Kennedy Park. In 2007 Galway came in at number eight on the world's sexiest city list.

Every September up to 10,000 people swarm into Galway for the Galway International Oyster Festival. This is one of the city's biggest festivals and fine wines, gourmet food and entertainment abound with copious quantities of oysters and Guinness of course. www.galwayoysterfest.com

For horse racing fans the racecourse is just a short distance from the town centre. Several race meetings are held every year with all the glitz and glamour that goes with this lifestyle. They even have their own Ladies Day and around 150,000 people attend the Summer Festival every year. www.galwayraces.com.

If you like horses visit the Ballinasloe International October Fair & Festival which is a country show that centres around everything equine. The nine day event has a community feeling and there is plenty to do and see. There is live music, food, arts and crafts and plenty to keep the children occupied. Join the 85,000 other people that go every year and have some fun.
www.ballinasloe.com

In July every year the Galway Arts Festival takes place with its famous Macnas parade. Macnas is a performance company based in Galway but has entertained audiences in 20 different countries across the globe. The name mean Joyful Abandonment in Irish and this is exactly what the company portray in their exuberant and colourful street performances every July. They have been credited with changing Ireland's view on public displays and at the Galway Arts Festival the streets get overcrowded as thousands flock to see the show.

Galway City has two theatres, the Druid Theatre and the Town Hall Theatre, that host a variety of events between them. They offer a full programme of theatre shows from local and visiting companies, comedy, music, readings and talks.

Location & Orientation

County Galway is in the Irish province of Connacht and is on the west coast of Ireland. After County Cork it is the largest county in Ireland and is home to a large Irish speaking population. In 2011 the population of the county was 250,500 and approximately 78% are white Irish, descendants of the Norman settlers and native Gaelic peoples. Around 17% are non-Irish and the remainder are foreign born Irish.

To get to County Galway there is a choice of car, coach or train or flying into Knock or Shannon Airports both about 50 miles away. The airport at Carnmore in Galway City closed in 2011 as the runway was too short to accommodate large commercial aircraft. Connemara airport to the west of the region has flights to the Aran Islands and Inis Bó Finne Island.

Most Galwegians use buses to get around both in the city and throughout the county. Several different bus companies operate the routes including scheduled services to Dublin, Dublin Airport, Limerick, Cork and Clifden. The main rail and bus station is Ceannt Station at Fairgreen in the heart of the city. Ceannt Station opened in 1851 and there is a proposed major development for the area including the station and the surrounding land.

Road links are good with three primary national roads. Plans are being made to develop the Galway-Dublin, Galway-Limerick and Galway-Tuam routes into dual carriageways or maybe motorways.

By sea there are regular freight and passenger ferry services between Galway and its various islands. Galway Harbour is earmarked for major development should funds be agreed.

Climate & When to Visit

County Galway has a fairly limited range of seasonal change of temperature. The city is a major tourist destination and experiences all four seasons but without the extremes found in some places. One sure thing about the Irish weather is that rain will fall at some point in every month of the year and quite heavily in the autumn months. There is some 90mm of rainfall in October.

The summer months see an average of around 18°C to 20°C with a fair amount of rain falling. In autumn the temperature drops quite quickly to 9°C in October and 5°C by November. The daytime high can be 14-16°C but mornings and evenings will definitely have a nip in the air. If you are lucky in winter the mercury might reach 7°C but is more likely to hover around the 2°C mark. January is the coldest month but once the month is out the temperature starts to rise quite quickly. By March it can be up to 12°C and as much as 15°C in April.

Spring is always a pleasant time to visit when the dampness of winter is leaving and the promise of warm summer days are just round the corner. A few layers of clothing are always the best idea as the sunny days can still be chilly when the sun disappears behind the clouds. Galway as a county very rarely used to see snow, frost and hail but with climate changes over recent years the possibility of this happening seems to increase as each year passes. If you plan to visit the county in the winter months make sure you have sufficiently warm clothing and some decent, snow proof footwear.

Sightseeing Highlights

Galway Bay & Salthill Promenade

Galway Bay is about 30 miles long and between and 6 and 18 miles wide. The best way to take in the stunning scenery is to go for a drive heading out from Galway City at the top of the bay. Head west towards Spiddal passing Barna Woods on your right and on the left you can listen to the sound of the sea crashing onto the rocks below.

There are plenty of side roads leading down to the cliffs with places to park so take your time and enjoy the fresh sea air. A good place to stop is just before the Loughinch River where there are good opportunities to take spectacular photos across the bay. If you head south from Galway City towards Kinvarra the road is more or less at sea level and the stone walls hold back verdant green fields. There are numerous inlets and rivers and some amazing views across to the Aran Islands.

If a walk sounds better than a drive then take a wander along the two mile long Salthill Promenade in Galway City. Overlooking Galway Bay the promenade is great for walking, jogging, cycling or rollerblading. There are benches along the way so take time to sit down and admire the views all the way across the County Clare. If you fancy a dip in the sea the Blackrock diving platform is still there. The platform is a left-over from when the area was a popular bathing spot in the 1950's and it is still used by a few brave souls to get into the sea rather than the safer method of the nearby steps.

Turoe Pet Farm & Leisure Park

Bullaun,
Loughrea,
County Galway,
Tel: +353 091 841 580
http://www.turoepetfarm.com

Turoe Farm opened in 1993 and is now one of the best visitor attractions in the west of Ireland.

The farm is family run and offers great value for money with excellent customer service. There is always something going on around the 14 acre park no matter what the weather conditions. Walk round the park and have a cuddle with the animals or have a go at feeding the young ones. There are friendly llamas and alpacas who will happily pose for photos as well as goats, sheep, donkeys and ponies. The pond is full of ducks and geese and don't forget to pay a visit to The Wishing Well.

If the weather is wet there is always Inflatable City, one of Europe's largest indoor bouncing castles, to keep the children amused. The Coffee Shop serves hot drinks and snacks and sells souvenirs while the Country Kitchen has a more extensive menu if you are feeling hungry. The opening times vary widely through the year but for summer time it is generally the end of May until the end of August from 10am to 7pm. For special times like Halloween and Christmas it is worth checking on their website. The admission fee is €12 for children and €6 for adults with family passes available.

Inis Bó Finne (Island of the White Cow)

County Galway,
Tel: +353 95 45 895
www.inishbofin.com

Inis Bó Finne or Island of the White Cow lies around seven miles off the coast of Galway.

Approximately 200 people live on the island at the present time and tourism is one of the main incomes on the island along with fishing and farming. Evidence shows that Inis Bó Finne has been inhabited since 8000-4000 BC and at one time the island was used a prison for Catholic priest. The island has its own Ceili band and often plays host to visiting artists and musicians.

Visitors can take mountain walks, go hill climbing, try shore angling or dive into the clear waters surrounding the island. The beaches have won awards for safety and the pristine sands are littered with shells waiting to be collected. A rather odd aspect of the island is that there are no trees at all. Over the years any wood was cut down for fuel and as the sea air is laden with salt the trees never managed to grow again

To get to Inis Bó Finne the ferry departs from Cleggan in the Connemara region and there are three crossings a day in summer and two in winter. A bus runs straight from Galway City to Cleggan each day. For staying on the island there are a range of hotels, B&B's, hostels and a few camping places as well as private house and apartment rentals. Most of the bigger hotels have restaurants and there are various other bars and places to eat. The community centre has a playgroup and sells a selection of books and items relating to the island.

Leisureland Galway

Salthill Promenade
Galway City
Tel: +353 91 521 455
www.leisureland.ie/

Leisureland is a multi-purpose leisure space in Galway
with three swimming pools, a 1000 seat venue and a high
tech gym. The leisure centre has won numerous awards
for customer service, safety and hygiene as well as
services for the disabled. The swimming area has great
facilities for everyone, a 25 metre pool for serious
swimmers is alongside a pirate ship and paddle boats for
the little ones. A 65 metre slide and giant inflatables add
to the fun for all to enjoy. The gym has all the equipment
for a good work out and there are many different fitness
classes. Opening times and prices do vary so it is best to
check online or call in advance.

Connemara National Park

Letterfrack, County Galway
Tel: +353 95 41 054
www.connemaranationalpark.ie/

Connemara National Park opened in 1980 and the 2,957
hectares is home to some of the famous mountains of
Beanna Beola or Twelve Bens range.

The whole area is rich in wildlife and there are miles of grasslands, woodlands, heaths and bogs to explore under the watchful eyes of Muckanaght, Benbrack, Benbaun and Bencullagh (a few of the Twelve Bens). The parklands were once owned by several private individuals as well as Kylemore Abbey Estate, the Letterfrack Industrial School and Richard Martin. Richard Martin, aka Humanity Dick, helped start the RSPCA in the 19th century. The Connemara National Park is now owned by the state and is solely for park purposes. Admission to the park is free and the grounds are open all year round. The Visitor Centre is open from March to October from 9am to 5.30pm daily.

Tropical Butterfly Centre

Carraroe
Connemara
County Galway

A couple of miles from Rossveale Harbour is the unique experience of the Tropical Butterfly Centre where the brightly coloured exotic butterflies fly free in a giant enclosed tropical garden. There are some very rare plants creating an atmosphere of lush splendour in this simulated natural environment. There is a small coffee shop with butterfly themed gifts and local crafts to purchase. The centre is open from May to September.

Aran Islands

http://www.aranislands.ie

The Aran Islands are a few miles off the County Clare coast at the entrance to Galway Bay. There are three islands, the smallest to the east is Inisheer, the middle one by location and size is Inishmaan and the largest one to the west is Inishmore or Aranmore. All the islanders speak Irish and the local language is used on many of the islands signs. Transport to the islands is by ferry or air and it is recommended to stay a few days to reap the benefits of the fresh air, culture and heritage. There are about 437 varieties of wild flowers across the islands and what better way to see them than by hiring a pushbike or take a tour in a pony and trap.

Coole Park National Nature Reserve

Coole Visitor Centre
Gort,
County Galway
Tel: +353 91 631 804
www.coolepark.ie/

Coole Park with Garryland covers an area of 405 hectares with about four mile of nature trails wandering through woods, limestone, furloughs and going past rivers and Coole Lake.

The Family Trail is an easy walk of a mile or so, going past the deer park, the site of the old house and ending at the Autograph Tree in the walled garden. The Seven Woods trail is a bit longer and goes through the woods made famous in the poems by W.B. Yeats. There are beautiful flowers and birds to look out for and depending on the time of year you could see butterflies and bluebells, violets and squirrels, treecreepers and swans.

The house was the home of the dramatist Lady Gregory and Coole Park was at the centre of the Irish Literary revival at the beginning of the 20th century. George Bernard Shaw and William Butler Yeats were frequent visitors and with many other literary greats they carved their initials into an old beech tree. The Autograph Tree is still standing but the actual house is long gone. The Visitor Centre is part of the old stable and across the cobbled yard are the remains of the harness and coach rooms.

Coole Park is open from Easter until the end of September from 10am to 5pm and an hour later in July and August. Admission is free, there are trail guide booklets, postcards, books and maps on sale and there is a tea room for a refreshing drink when you have wandered round the grounds.

Kylemore Abbey & Victorian Walled Gardens

Kylemore, Connemara, County Galway
Tel: +353 95 41146
www.kylemoreabbeytourism.ie/

Kylemore Abbey is stunning; there is no other word for it. Set against a backdrop of a beautiful forest with the water of Pollacapul Lough moving serenely in front, the Abbey is the stuff that fairy tales are made of. There is far more to see than just the Abbey and six acres of Victorian Walled Gardens will keep even the most avid gardener happy for hours and the beautiful Gothic church with its sad story will delight visitors.

A visit to Kylemore Abbey is a great family day out and there is a restaurant and tea room serving homemade dishes, a craft shop for picking up some locally made gifts as well as guided tours of the abbey and ample photo opportunities. There is a special play trail for children designed by local students. Throughout the abbey and grounds there are 22 pieces of play equipment made from the fallen wood of the estate trees and each telling a Kylemore story.

The abbey has been home to a group of Benedictine Nuns since 1920 and it is the only such community in Ireland. Some of the abbey is open to visitors who wish to see inside and the short tour takes in some of the rooms that have been restored since a fire in 1959 damaged much of the interior. Not all of the abbey can be viewed as the nuns live in the abbey and in return take great pride in looking after parts of the Victorian Walled Garden.

Kylemore Abbey is open all the year round and adults pay €12.50, OAP's €10 and students €9. For children under ten years old admission is free. There are various family passes available and if you book online a 10% discount applies.

Battle of Aughrim Interpretative Centre

Galway-Dublin Road (N6)
Aughrim
Ballinasloe
County Galway
Tel: +353 90 967 3939

The Battle of Aughrim tool place in July, 1961 and 9,000 of the 45,000 soldiers involved lost their lives. The course of European and Irish history was changed that day when William of Orange fought James II of England.

The centre is right next to the battlefield and it is easy to relive the sights and sounds of that day through the advent of modern technology. There is a café, bookshop and craft shop to visit as well and the opening times are Tuesday to Saturday 10am to 6pm. Ticket price is €5 for adults, €4 for students and OAP's, €3 for children and a family ticket can be purchased for €12.

Galway City Museum

Galway City Museum
Spanish Parade
Galway City
Tel: 353 91 532 460
www.galwaycitymuseum.ie/

Galway City Museum aims to preserve the history of the city and provide a space where locals and visitors can come and learn about Galway past and present. There are three floors telling the story of the city from mediaeval times to the present day, including an exhibition on the Claddagh village. Two local children have created a special Kids Museum Detective sheet so if you are visiting with children make sure they use their super-sleuthing skills on the way round. The museum is closed Sunday and Monday but open 10am to 5pm Tuesday to Saturday. Admission is free.

Corrib Princess River Cruise

Woodquay
Galway City
Tel: +353 91 592 447
www.corribprincess.ie/

Take a 90 minute relaxing river cruise on the Corrib Princess and admire the natural beauty of the waterways of River Corrib and Lough Corrib. Pass by castles standing proudly on the river banks, fishermen waiting for the catch of the day and swans vying for river space with canoeists.

The Corrib Princess is well equipped and the bar has good selection of drinks and some delicious Irish coffees. There is seating inside and out, toilets on board and the skipper points out all the most interesting points as you glide gently past. An adult ticket is €15, students and OAP's €13, children €7 and a family ticket of two adults and up to three children is €35.

Galway Cathedral

University and Gaol Roads, Cathedral Square
Galway City
Tel: + 353 91 563 577
www.galwaycathedral.ie/

Galway Cathedral has the distinction of being Europe's youngest stone cathedral, as it was constructed in the 1950's when similar buildings were being made out of concrete.

The cathedral has a rather impressive variety of art with a mosaic of the crucifixion and a statue of the Virgin. The details are mainly Gothic and Romanesque with a little bit of Renaissance added in. The cathedral is open from 8am to 6pm each day and a donation is asked for rather than a fixed entrance fee.

Recommendations for the Budget Traveller

Places to Stay

Barnacles Hostel

10 Quay Street, Latin Quarter, Galway
Tel: +353 91 568 644
www.barnacles.ie/

In the heart of Galway in the Latin Quarter is Barnacles Hostel where there are often festivals and dancing happening right outside.

The hostel is close to all the major attractions like Eyre Square, The Claddagh and the Spanish Arch. Quay Street is pedestrianised and there is a buzzing café and restaurant atmosphere that can enjoyed along with a pint of Guinness or two.

The hostel has 112 beds in a mixture of private rooms and shared dorms, with female only dorms available. The room prices start from €10 per night and this includes breakfast. There is free Wifi, 24 hour reception, a self-catering kitchen and laundry facilities. The reception staffs are friendly and will give advice on the best places to visit and can even book tickets for certain attractions.

If you want to get away without paying at Barnacles Hostel for your bed for the night all you have to do is perform for your fellow guests. Singers and musicians can get free accommodation if they are entertaining enough. There are other events as well where free accommodation can be won.

Galway City Hostel

Frenchville Lane, Eyre Square, Galway
Tel: +353 91 566 959
www.galwaycityhostel.com/

There are great views of Eyre Square from the Galway City Hostel and fantastic transport links.

The hostel is opposite the main bus and train station so getting around couldn't get any easier. There are always fellow travellers to share stories with over a beer or two or maybe plan some outings together.

The hostel has comfortable and solid beds and the bathrooms are bright and clean with plenty of hot water. There is a fully equipped self-catering kitchen if you fancy cooking up your own grub and the hostel supplies free tea and coffee all day. If you want to relax there is free TV and a selection of DVD's plus board games and free internet. Guests are offered a light breakfast to get the day off to a good start and this is included in the room rates from €15. The accommodation is in eight bedded mixed dorms. There is a 24 hour reception and they can book discounted tickets for various bus tours and ferry trips.

Lakeshore House

Ballard
Clonbur
County Galway
Tel: +353 94 954 831
www.lakeshoreconnemara.com/

Just 50 metres from the shores of Lake Corrib is the aptly named Lakeshore B&B. It is a quick five minute drive from the village of Clonbur and only 15 minutes from the Connemara region with Lough Mask, Lough Nafooey and Joyce Valley.

The house sits in rock gardens, all beautifully designed, with garden chairs for relaxing and a children's play area. There is plenty of free car parking and even a jetty with boats for hire. If the weather is not quite so good there is a pleasant lounge to relax in where there is a piano to play or a guitar to strum.

All the rooms are en-suite with hair dryers and free Wifi. Choose from double, twin or family or there is a family apartment as well. The rooms cost from €35 per person per night with various offers for longer stays. Children under 12 sharing with their parents receive a 25% discount. A full Irish breakfast is served and there is a menu to choose your favourite items from.

Árd Einne Guesthouse

Inis Mór
Aran Islands
County Galway
Tel: +353 99 61126
www.ardeinnearan.com/

Árd Einne Guesthouse has its very own beach so walking along the coastline is a great way to explore, taking in the views across to the Clare and Galway coastlines in the distance. Situated on the east side of the island the village of Kilronan is only two kilometres away where you can visit the local pub and listen to traditional Irish music.

The guesthouse had been a family business for more than 30 years and the hosts will share with you all the best places to visit on the island. The island of Inishmore is the largest of the three Aran Islands and access is by boat or small plane.

There are eight en-suite rooms all with free Wifi, a hairdryer and a hospitality tray plus a stunning sea view so waking up is always a pleasure. A traditional Irish breakfast will set you up for the day and vegetarian or special diets can be catered for. Evening meals are available as well and can be prepared while you relax in the lounge with a glass of wine. Expect to pay from €60 per night for two people sharing a twin room including breakfast.

Oak Lodge Portumna

St Brendan's Road,
Portumna,
County Galway,
Tel: +353 90 974 1549
www.oaklodgeportumna.ie/

In the east of County Galway is the River Shannon and this is where you will find the Oak Lodge. Portumna is a busy town all year round and there is always something happening. The Shorelines Arts Festival is held every year in the town which will be of great interest to anyone who likes poetry, prose, sculptures and paintings. For more active types there is hurling, cycling, swimming and running.

The River Shannon and Lough Derg are all on the doorstep for fishing and there are many more fishing hotspots within a short drive. For fishermen staying at Oak Lodge there is a fridge, drying room and a free laundry service.

Oak Lodge has five rooms, all en-suite and the prices range from €25-€35 per person per night and this includes breakfast. The rooms all have TV, a hairdryer, hospitality tray and free Wifi. A self-catering option at €20 per person per night is also available and there is a kitchen for guests to use. There are double, twin, family and single rooms to choose from.

Places to Eat & Drink

Breathnachs Bar

The Square
Oughterard
County Galway
Tel: +353 091 552 818

Breathnachs Bar is a great place for good value and tasty pub grub. They also serve breakfast, not just a full Irish with plenty of home-baked bread but delicious pancakes dripping with maple syrup. The food is simple but freshly cooked and the owner is very hands-on so the bar is well run and always busy. The dinner menu is varied and the service excellent. Food is available Monday to Sunday lunchtimes 12 noon to 3pm and evenings 6pm to 9.30pm.

Pedro's Cafe & Grill

Tuam Shopping Centre
Tuam
County Galway
Tel: +353 93 52663
www.cafetuam.com/

This is a great place for breakfast, lunch or dinner. It is a good family friendly restaurant and the choice is great from traditional breakfasts to super salads and fresh grilled meats, pizza and pasta. An unusual item is the fried egg sandwich with cheese and chicken, served with coleslaw and chips. It isn't on the menu but they will cook it by special request. There is a very tempting dessert menu and freshly ground coffee to finish your meal with. The hours are limited as it is in the Tuam shopping centre, Monday to Saturday 9am to 7pm and Sunday 12 noon to 6pm

The Forge Pub & Eatery

Moycullen Village.
County Galway
Tel: +353 91 868 944
www.theforgepubmoycullen.com/

In the heart of Moycullen village is the Forge Pub and Eatery. This is a very popular spot with locals and tourists alike and can get busy but as they have entertainment it is no hardship to wait a while for your food.

The pub is warm and inviting and the staff are friendly and families are welcome. A full Irish breakfast is €8 and main courses start at €7.50 for lunches and €13.50 for dinner. The Forge Pub and Eatery is open for breakfast Monday to Saturday 9.30am -12 noon and then from lunchtime through to dinner from 12 noon to 9pm every day.

The Bard's Den

Letterfrack,
Connemara
County Galway
Tel: +353 954 1042
www.bardsden.com

The Bard's Den is well known for not just the food they serve but as a place to go for socialising and seisúns. A seisún is maybe what the English call a jamming session where the local musicians go to make music and have a good time. In winter the fires are roaring and anytime of the year the pub's beautiful collie dog will always be pleased to see you.

Beautiful local produce, Connemara lamb, fresh seafood and Irish beef are all turned into the most wonderful home cooked traditional pub meals. The all-day menu is from €3.50 for a starter and €12.75 for a main course with a variety of daily specials. There is a good range of drinks and wines are reasonable prices to accompany the meal.

Cupán Tae

8 Quay Lane
Galway
Tel: +353 189 5000
www.cupantae.eu/

Cupán Tae is one of the stalwarts of Galway dining experiences. Everything is top class, the sweets, cakes and pastries are to die for and the service and atmosphere are perfect. There is a fantastic selection of loose leaf teas, 30 in total, and on top of all that everything is reasonably priced.

One of the specials is "Eggs Benny" so make sure you try it. For those with a savoury tooth there is a selection of salads, jacket potatoes and other non-sugary goodies to sample. Cupán Tae is open Monday to Thursday 10am to 5pm, Friday and Saturday 10am to 6pm and Sunday 11am to 6pm.

Places to Shop

Penneys

Eyre Square Shopping Centre, Galway
Tel: +353 91 566 889
www.primark.ie

Cheap and cheerful and sometimes untidy is the best way to describe Penneys.

The company has 257 stores across Europe and employs 45,000 people. Penneys will be best known to many people as Primark. Everything in a Penneys store is good value, sort of like a year round sale. The styles are always up to the minute and it is very hard to visit any branch and come out without buying something. There are clothes for all the family as well as items for the home.

The Eyre Square branch is open Monday to Wednesday 9am to 7pm, Thursday and Friday 9am to 9pm, Saturday 9am to 7pm and Sunday 11am to 7pm.

Fallers Sweater Shop

25 High Street
Galway City
Tel: +353 91 564 833

Fallers Sweater Shop is a brilliant place to go for some genuine good quality touristy gifts. There is a wide selection of jumpers and knitted items for all the family and even if you don't really mean to buy anything, you probably will. There is plenty of cute Guinness memorabilia as well as cups, mugs, postcards and many other souvenirs.

Royal Tara

Connolly Ave, Mervue, Galway
Tel: +353 91 705 602
www.royal-tara.com/

If you love china this is definitely the place to visit. There are some beautiful gift ideas, for yourself as well as friends. Choose from Celtic crafts and bone china plates and cups, carved wooden trinket boxes and ceramic or glass trinkets. The staff are friendly and very helpful and there is a shipping service if you are far away from home and need your purchases sent on.

Ceardlann-Spiddal Craft & Design Studios

15 Km/11 Miles west of Galway city
www.ceardlann.com/

Ceardlann is a craft village a short drive from Galway city centre and is home to 10 different craft workers who design, create and sell their own work. There are paper crafts, ceramics, coins, basket weaving, beautiful hand woven tapestries and shawls, jewellery and lamps made from glass and a range of paintings using acrylics. The Builín Blasta Café serves a delicious selection of sweet and savoury snacks and meals and a very tempting range of hand-made chocolates.

Thomas Dillon Claddagh Gold

1 Quay Street
Galway
Tel: +353 91 566 365
www.claddaghring.ie

This is the original home of the Claddagh ring and at the back of the shop there is a tiny museum which tells the history of this legendary piece of Irish jewellery. Take care if you have a rucksack though as it can knock things over. The Thomas Dillon shop has been in existence since 1750 and is the only maker of the Original Claddagh ring with the official Irish Assay mark stamped on each ring.

The Claddagh ring or Love and Friendship ring has a long history behind it dating back to the 16th century and this is all explained in the museum. Most people nowadays don't know the whole history and the ring is generally given as a token of love and affection. How the ring is worn can tell a great deal about a person. If the heart is towards the fingernails the wearer is unattached, but if the crown is pointing upwards the fingernails the wearer is in love or married.

The shop has a great range of rings to suit all ages and budgets and if the size isn't quite correct it can be resized while you wait. There are bracelets, lockets and earrings to choose from as well as brooches and cufflinks.

13207093R00024

Printed in Great Britain
by Amazon.co.uk, Ltd.,
Marston Gate.